LOVABLE DOGS/ PERROS ADORABLES

By Katie Kawa   Traducción al español: Eduardo Alamán

Gareth Stevens
Publishing

Please visit our website, www.garethstevens.com. For a free color catalog of all our high-quality books, call toll free 1-800-542-2595 or fax 1-877-542-2596.

Library of Congress Cataloging-in-Publication Data

Kawa, Katie.
  [Lovable dogs. Spanish & English]
  Lovable dogs = Perros adorables / Katie Kawa.
     p. cm. — (Pet corner = Rincón de las mascotas)
  Includes index.
  ISBN 978-1-4339-5595-2 (library binding)
  1. Dogs—Juvenile literature. I. Title. II. Title: Perros adorables.
  SF426.5.K3918 2011
  636.7—dc22

                                            2011003606

First Edition

Published in 2012 by
Gareth Stevens Publishing
111 East 14th Street, Suite 349
New York, NY 10003

Copyright © 2012 Gareth Stevens Publishing

Editor: Katie Kawa
Designer: Andrea Davison-Bartolotta
Spanish Translation: Eduardo Alamán

Photo credits: Cover, pp. 5, 7, 9, 11, 13, 17, 19, 21, 23, 24 (coat, paws) Shutterstock.com; p. 1 iStockphoto.com; pp. 15, 24 (bone) Chris Amaral/Photodisc/Thinkstock.

Printed in the United States of America

CPSIA compliance information: Batch #CS11GS: For further information contact Gareth Stevens, New York, New York at 1-800-542-2595.

Contents

- -

Contenido

A dog wags its tail.
It is happy.

El perro menea la cola.
El perro está contento.

Dogs learn many
fun tricks. They like
to roll over.

Los perros aprenden
muchos trucos divertidos.
A los perros les gusta
tumbarse y dar vueltas.

A dog has lots of fur.
This is called a coat.

Los perros tienen mucho
pelo. Al pelo de los perros
se le llama pelaje.

A person brushes a dog's coat. This keeps it soft.

Una persona cepilla el pelaje de un perro. Así lo mantiene suave.

A dog has a wet nose. This helps it smell very well.

Los perros tienen la naríz húmeda. Esto les ayuda a oler muy bien.

13

A dog chews a bone.
It cleans its teeth.

Este perro mastica un
hueso. Así se limpia
los dientes.

A dog has four feet.
They are called paws.

Los perros tienen
cuatro patas.

A dog needs to play
every day.

Los perros necesitan
jugar todos los días.

A dog plays fetch.
A person throws a ball
and the dog brings
it back.

Este perro juega a la
pelota. Una persona
lanza la pelota y el
perro se la devuelve.

Dogs love to play outside!

¡A los perros les encanta jugar afuera!

23

Words to Know/ Palabras que debes saber

bone/
(el) hueso

coat/
(el) pelaje

paws/
(las) patas

Index / Índice